MW01258621

Nioque of the Early-Spring

Nioque of the Early-Spring

Francis Ponge

Translated by Jonathan Larson

The Song Cave

Published by The Song Cave, 2018
www.the-song-cave.com

Design and layout by Mary Austin Speaker

ISBN 978-0-9988290-3-6
Library of Congress Control Number: 2018930692

FIRST EDITION

TABLE OF CONTENTS

TRANSLATOR'S INTRODUCTION

> *"... for want of language and the novelty of things"*
>
> *"thus, our age is unable to look back on the lifetime before, but where reason shows a trace."*
>
> Lucretius, *On the Nature of Things,*
> from *Book I* and *Book V*

> *"I was speaking of spring. This forest decided to speak of you, but why did it decide to speak of you? Because it is spring. A forest begins to express itself in spring."*
>
> Francis Ponge, *Oral Tentative*

The work of Francis Ponge is formed by the firm, lucid, and sound. His most widely lauded collection of poems, *Le Parti Pris des Choses* (translated into English as *The Nature of Things, The Voice of Things, On the Side of Things, Siding with Things,* and, most recently, *Partisan of Things*), appeared initially in 1942 and established Ponge as a leading voice in French poetry. With its celebratory and playful paeans to everyday objects like mollusks, moss, and fruit crates, the poet elaborated a reinvention of the prose-poem in which the subjects are held in common with the fibrous ligature of their textural make-up.

This collection of notes, *Nioque de l'Avant-Printemps*, gathered over the course of a several weeks stay in the countryside during the first part of April 1950, builds out the earlier rhetorical platforms, but with an expansive glance toward seasonal (or serial) time itself as the subject, and more so its eternal return, a mode hinted at in *The Nature of Things* with the two poems *The cycle of the seasons* and *The end of autumn*. As explained in the opening note to the reader, 'nioque' comes into play as a neologism that draws on various Latin and Greek root forms of gnossos (knowledge), while the early-spring connotes the liminal phase in anticipation of the time to come, "when after the several months of silence it vomits green" (*Oral Tentative*, Francis Ponge). The echoing of 'note' in 'nioque' sounds out the new approach to Ponge's poetic, as committed documentation with the concern not only of transmitting knowledge, but also of knowing again, which is to say that in knowing a thing one already looks forward to knowing the thing again, if one (as Ponge did) takes the words of Lucretius seriously "that any thing thus cannot return to nothing." The matter that is, is the matter: adapting, altering, and renewing itself, in the orchard as within the circulations of speech, art, and letters, to carry on flowering, threading, and spreading (while "smiling at another") by their diverse mutual delight.

Ponge will thus ascribe this text's politic to the 'events of 1968,' the spring of its earliest publication, as "something to return to." Though historical time is made, and marked, by political actors, the artist is reintroduced as the capacity to remake and remark upon the past in advance of its future. All the more fitting that this text would delve into the failings of the French Communist Party as if to say *there the speech rang hollow – here the hollow rings with speech.* It is in this context that *Nioque de l'Avant-Printemps* was written, three years before the poet, who suffered from mild aphasia, accepted an invitation to give a rare talk, entitled *La Tentative Orale*, and contemporaneously with what will appear as the chapter *Murmur: (Condition and Destiny of the Artist)* in another work *Méthodes*, dated in the manuscripts from April 2 to July 18 of 1950. Speech as such (and alternatively, keeping mute) is the concern here, both of the season and of the poet-artist, whose murmured speech comes out as the green emission to make an inward thing outwardly known, the pushing out of stems and leaves that show what's held at their core, when, in fact (or in the act), it's never been better concealed by all the foliating overgrowth. The early-spring ushers in the twofold season when the heart of matter prepares for coming *into* and *out of* its own, simultaneously, to dwell within a shared plane as music. Here the poet consorts with the abundant and abounding elemental particularities that take on their shape, as one speaks:

"You...

You are there, all around me – today, you trees, pebbles of the orchard, clouds in the sky, wondrous dead nature, uncontested nature."

The voice inhabits the middle distance, as it were, between the addressed object and the speaker tasked with vocalizing these to an audience, therein committing to an alliance that is partial, in every sense:

"We will speak to them, to humans.

So, to take on their voice, their speech. Let us speak! You speak! I am your interpreter. Say what you have to say. Say only what you are." It is imperative that things are spoken, that the world of things express itself (its mute nature), but without hyperbole. The poet and artist is called upon to do but this.

We start into the text by positioning ourselves to the south, facing the Mediterranean ("even the Aegean"), in a farmhouse while taking note of the wind driving in storm clouds from the west (i.e. the right, both directionally and politically). This concern with situating oneself runs through the four sections, and closes with the reclamation of the same opening viewpoint: "We look to midday readily; / Our dramatics come to us westerly." The midday would signal the end of the humanist age when humans would retake their place within, and not atop, the natural world. Oblique reference is made to cooled friendships with P and S (written out as Paulhan and Sartre in the manuscript, which Jean-Marie Gleize and Bernard Veck make note of in the Pléiade edition) who were at that time delegating back and forth the responsibilities of publishing a collection of tributary pieces to Ponge, a proposal to collect funds for him that was Sartre's initially. Concerns of taking side are further embedded in this text upon its republication, having already been split up between the opposing attitudes of the two journals *L'Éphémère* and *Tel quel* in which excerpts of *Nioque* had appeared. To the former magazine, whose aim it was to delimit a purer poetry and reclaim it as the privileged genre, Ponge sent the selection *capital proem* to put forward the notion of the poet as a researcher, a worker who cedes the floor to the armoire, while to the latter, under the editorship of Philippe Sollers and representing a post-structural inquiry suspicious of the claims made under the flag of art and poetry, he submitted the pieces demonstrating the kinship of the artist and writer who fills their canvas with the material landscape present so as to interveniently portray the poet to both journals as the consummate revolutionary for carrying onward the efforts of preserving the harmonious simultaneity of all things.

The *canevas* is foregrounded as the conceptacle of time in this booklet, figuring as the leaves to turn and pass back over, their surfaces absorbing the dimensions of color and the winds of inspiration, making music. In the section titled *Proem* we come across the declaration that "to woven cloth, god sends the thread," a modification of the saying "to woven web, God sends the thread," a proverb that Ponge undoubtedly came across in the Littré dictionary (an urtext to Ponge's poetic) under the entry for 'ourdi' (the past participle of to weave). Concomitant with trading out the web for paintable cloth, the lowercase god is chosen to replace the upper, perhaps as a thing among things, a Spinozan god. We also find this subtle exchange with an uncharacteristic capitalization of *Music* to conclude section III and at the end of COLD WINTER RAIN OR EARLY-SPRING where "all of mute nature or (interested or disinterested) says April over and again," though the names of months take the lowercase in French and elsewise in the text. These majuscule and minuscule letterings return around the order of things, as if to say that one achieves the proper noun but by delight in onself. Ponge expresses his disdain for the "nefarious Jerusalem-Athens-Rome axis" in a conversation with Serge Gavronsky due to its implementation of the

Platonic project that was responsible for propping up *humanity* as the unit to govern the state of things by, and would rather swap the one Christian God for the Epicurean (pagan) spirit and "the living nature of its *diverse* divinities." The manifold presences of regeneration return again, but with difference, announced every revolving calendar year with "the frigid worries" and "the bluish overshadowing" blowing in from the west. This "bad weather" is but a "passing meanness" however, and necessary for the restart, to obliterate "bars, gates, cages, damp prisons of which nothing will remain!" when rejoining the chorus to "resay April" (or March, or October, or November, for that matter) "so that all of nature says it over and again." As Ponge stressed in an early poem that takes up Paul Claudel's polysemous trope *Co-naissance*: "it is not so much about *connaître* (knowing) as it is about *naître* (coming to be, or being born)" (La Loi et les Prophètes). One returns to the renewed page of the book by saying April again, acknowledging the liberational force coming together at its source (we might think of the double-forged adjective *reinentsprungenes* (purelysprung) that Hölderlin coined to describe the Rhine river), restoring the hydrological cycle so that "through all the pores (faucets) liberty springs forth." I have retained the French word douix mentioned in the section COLD WINTER RAIN OR EARLY-SPRING because of its regional association for a rocky crevice whose etymology derives from the Celtic term for fountain or spring, and with origins associated with the Gaulish deity Divona, a sacred spring. Because the poet artist lends their voice to the eternally recurrent streams of time and weather (the double-sense of *le temps* conveys both *weather* and *time*), they hold with their emancipatory charge, their "elemental meanness" that is always still coming into formation, both as "cold winter rain" and the bourgeoning "early-spring," alongside the natural order of the material world, whose borders and confinements of human imposition are thus broken down and apart, to take on the textum as it is given.

SEPTEMBER 21 2017

J.L

TO THE READER

Nioque of the Early-Spring was first published in part, under this title, in the review *L'Éphémère* n° 2 (April 1967), page 49 to 59, and in part in the review *Tel quel* n° 33 (spring 1968), page 3 to 17, under the title *The Early-Spring.*

NIOQUE is the phonetic writing (as one could write *iniorant*) of GNOQUE, the word I coined from the Greek root meaning *knowledge*, thus not so as to rework Satie's GNOSSIENNE nor Claudel's CON-NAISSANCE (of the East).

The first publication of this text, though it had been written long before, had curiously preceded the "events" of Berkeley, Berlin or Paris by very little in 1967 and 1968, considered by some as *Spring*, in imitation of contemporary events like the "Prague Spring", e.g.

F. P.

I

LES FLEURYS, SUNDAY APRIL 2 1950.

Farmhouse, of a single elongate ground floor, facing south. Protected by several outbuildings that form perpendicular wings, to the right.

Westerly, that is to say from the right, coming in bursts, cutting close at the ground to high up among the airs even, often in gusts, hailstones, the frigid worries, the bluish overshadowing.

Savage and enthusiastic mood held under sunlight, around ten in the morning, as under a frosted headlamp, very high to the left, which lays bare the festoons of cloud and suddenly discovers itself, with a laugh along the façades.

They lean over the vegetation, letting drops of water onto the grass and into the branches.

We have one of the landscapes of the western septentrion there, all swept with water, always under the polar rag, the Atlantic mop-cloth.

... These storms a little colder than they are mild.

There the woods are thriving, so it is necessary to cut and dry its logs—they in turn will become roseate —so as to have a little fire in the ground floor fire-place of the house,—a little of this live coal's warmth coming from the wood lit by human industry to off-set the head colds and rheumatisms.

But underneath, nourishing, the elongate body of the brown earth.

•

It is on us to resay *November* as one opens a drawer (overfilled with pearls and old scarves), that spills itself (and pours out its overflow).

March has made its way here as one shakes the rags out a last time, as one makes a last pass with the sarp-cloth.

But the broideries quickly take their place again – the canvas fills at full speed.

Starting off from the old canvas, the broideries that grow out of the earth, the threads that grow out of the earth and knot themselves and (circulate) (progress) (amble) unravel themselves and spin and weave themselves, knit themselves,

form fringes, tassels, bobbles, braidlets.

Always too many (cherry blossoms), *for* the wind tears some off and scatters them. And enough of them must remain

so that the seeds are formed, the seeds, the little bobbins that bury themselves to be unraveled next spring.

But it also forms sticklets for the new canvas.

From these knots the animals are detached, spared, vagabonded (birds, insects, mammals, rodents and others).

The body of carbon variations, OUR body, from the black to the brown, to the green, and on to all the colors, even the white flowers, those diamonds.

Flowers imitating also the crystals of other rocks (all the colors imitate precious stones), and the flesh tones (of animals), and blood.

Meanwhile the (tender) women traffic in tepid water, the soups, the lyes; washing; heating the soup to nourish the warm bodies in their charge.

Wringing. Wiping.

And there is a music of the wash. Timbales of basins and pans, triangles of utensils.

And the big blue and white earthenware bowl of the skies finds itself all washed, all rinsed, all clean

and the looks turn blue, light up.

One smiles at another.

Yet the floor or wall clock beats the measure of the heart and of time (of the grave, of the despairing flight of time).

•

All comes to pass (we age), but the children climb the steps (of the staircase) of time to come laughing into the dining room.

Music of kisses. Birdsongs. Repopulation. Music of the kettle, of frying.

Music of fires. Crackling of the embers and logs. Bellows, streams of smoke.

•

Windows and mirrors cleaned, rubbed. One smiles at another.

II
PROEM OF THE SAME DAY

LES FLEURY, SUNDAY APRIL 2 1950.

At every instant to have lost, to have to refind one's vocabulary, to have to start over from the most common vocabulary, crude, down to earth, from the *lack* of vocabulary, nearly absolute, of farmers, of workers, of their badges, muddy, *earthen* blunder: look at what is good! Good sign. A chance.

(Not merely the vocabulary of the hay dock, but the *lack* of vocabulary.)

•

Like never-ending rain, the inclement weather brings decay, it deteriorates rustic houses, one must redress (repair) this or soon suffer collapse. Look at what is good. Good sign. This struggle, this elementary inclement weather. Rain, which damages, which brings walls to collapse, which rots the wood but also washes, that is healthy. Struggling with that, that is good. There is need for a constant reinvention; of the solid, of the good, of the roughly constituted.

So, one restarts to clear the throat or gullet, of pebbles, of the piles of pebbles in the road, of the earth and the water of the streams (that come from the rains).

As there are piles of pebbles collected in places to regravel the roads, surely there are words. One must go and search for them. In the gullet, in the gullet of others, in books, in dictionaries. By the shovelful, in scraping the graveling.

•

Countryside, encumbering solitude. It must be said that I sleep a lot, do not talk much, am rather grumbly, surly. No ideas, no readings, a real wild child. And that I cumber my body like an old tree-trunk of gnarled meat, of indigestible things at times, that I have plenty of mucus, catarrh, not the body that is unduly liberated, the spirit so numb and misty and dripping that it suddenly suns itself. That, that is good.

And the idea of death, the possibility of dying (from a gust of wind) at every instant that sweeps across me. That, that is good, too.

•

Landscape.

I like these large sooted knots, these expressions of knotted trunks, bundles of wet (soaked) firewood, large sooted knots under a grey silken sky (a little blue, made blue), and this untidying, these face-slaps of inclement weather (by the elements) in solitude.

The bistre darkens more and more, almost to black, from which the tender green suddenly suddenly surges (and even, at first, for the hawthorns, the white), then all the colors in imitation of the mineral.

It is from the branchlets, from the nearly black reglets that the green and the white surge up.

•

Electricity: the reddening filaments.

III

LES FLEURYS, THURSDAY APRIL 6 1950

After a cold and cloudy morning, and as for my head, a violent migraine...

All that cleared up around midday (as for me by an aspirin) (The sun played the aspirin for the sky, for nature),

Look at how around 17 h 30 the sky totally cleared, but the sun already low to the left barely giving off warmth,

I REREAD (and title) *the LANDSCAPE OF EARLY-SPRING* and I write that which follows, as preface-reflection:

"I am not able to say, write (or think) but what the season inspires me to."

(These days here: *landscapes, nioque, proems, notes of the early-spring.*)

•

One should gather all of this, and say it in fewer words.

In a way that is more concisely concrete, and thus nearly abstract (for the future).

•

To note that only several degrees of heat are lacking.

Hands almost cold. Patches of strong winds in places that the light will shape in several weeks.

Even more than the sun, it is patches of cold wind that mold the body.

•

Look where we are, the features of this season, the early-spring:

Between the need to make fire

(red fireside by the hearth or stove)

—and the possibility, thanks to certain sunny clearings (but due to a still cold wind), to not do anything at all and enjoy the sun.

•

In several days it will be too late, we will be at ease, the comforts of true spring (sunny. Fire having become useless). We will have forgotten this sensation (emotion). We are no longer able to say anything about it.

So, will it be necessary to wait for the next year to retake these notes and finish the picture?

No, it is necessary to complete it (in stride) immediately. But the courage? The contention of spirit (while the migraine...)?...and the pleasure of expression...?

To have not but what is to do! and lots of energy! of power of exertion. That is what should be done.

•

To pick up again with a jolt of energy right in the center of the sod and to mold it.

The sod of primary elements, of passions, eternal:

Rain, squirting, stinging, oblique features, damp, a destruction by unsolid traits, lizards, damaging the walls.

The cold rain of winter signifies sharp wet stings, a healthy nastiness, the struggle against it.

Sooted knots, knotted sticks in the smoke, worries, bluish overshadowing

Sun (light under frosted ceiling, skylight)

Threads unwind from underground and rapidly broider (flower buds and blossoms), the apple-trees, pear-trees, etc., the hawthorns.

Etc., etc.

COLD WINTER RAIN OR EARLY-SPRING.

LES FLEURYS, APRIL 7 1950.

The adversity, the oblique elementary meanness pierces with little liquid stingers even more supple than whip-strands (the rain, the whips), raining heavily from above, and healthy (unburdening, unbridling, liberating, satisfying dire worries; liberating voluminous worries generally coming westerly).

The cold adversity, the elemental meanness remade from the sand, from the gravel, from the bed of the brook with the walls of houses and with the walls of enclosures, healthy as by the struggle it is bound to lead against it, refreshing; recooling and reinvigorating all the same.

One does not die from it. It is only a benign meteor; yet able to to cause diseases, that are sometimes serious.

Hollows out cupules and sometimes pierces and damages, creating miniscule scree.

This cold rain, it is good. It is good that this

elementary degradation comes about, these little elementary depredations, this degradation of walls. To render back to the earth that which comes from it, that which had been taken from it, and to require rebuilding, sealing; to give us enjoyment from this bit of gravel, this gravelle.

To refill the cisterns.

To remoisten the fields, the labors.

A good deal for the feet of the trees. Instillations at the feet of the trees and the grass, like an eye-drop at the corner of the eye.

Renders the earth as plastic (made from the mud).

Lays out subterranean spreads; streams (streaming), douix, rivers, vauclusian fountains.

All this comes from a tartness, from a little (bad weather) passing meanness (passage of voluminous worries, coming first from ecstasy, from the evaporation of the sea).

•

Whips, arrows, stingers, swords, javelins, thorns of which nothing remains! Slaps, choleric outbursts, spit of which nothing will remain! Healthy displeasures, adversity, disagreements of which nothing will remain! Bars, gates, cages, damp prisons of which nothing will remain!

•

What then are you talking to us about, about humans, and do you believe that this interests us, so that it is on us to resay *April*, so that all of nature says it over and again (so that there are more seas than earth and still more fields than cities, than roads)
...that all of mute nature (interested and disinterested) still says April yet again.

BEGINNING OF THE POEM OF EARLY-SPRING.

Here, where the human, reduced to their just proportions, ...

A city, a big capital, in the corner of the landscape, like an abandoned cauldron, makes no more noise than a cauldron on the refuse heap.

The swarms of flying fortresses are able to pass. Soon no more than a flick of them remains. Unmoved nature to humans, you ridiculously complain to yourselves (Lamartine, Vigny, Hugo).

And all those of the now, to win money and fame, still say this (the "Just", the… this, that).

Alright then! Fortunately, it is unmoved! All the better!

This makes humans unmoved, since it is in the hearts of certain humans.

Besides, the nature in France is still yourselves: industrialized, commercialized; gardens, sufferings, labors, made of wood. However, liberty and the wind and the birds scutter there, they dance there at their ease;

Through all the pores (faucets) liberty springs forth.

LES FLEURYS, APRIL 8 1950.

What attracted us to the P.C. at first was the revolt against the living conditions made for humans, the taste of virtue and the thirst of devotion to a cause grandiose enough. After that it was the disgust of sordid protections, of humanitarian bleatings, of socialist verbosity and compromise (S.F.I.O).

The sentiment as to the exactions of *capitalism* should be opposed by methods at once energetic and supple, realistically, without illusions. We found, or believed to have found this in the Bolsheviks. The freeing of a serious sort, they seemed to us (set free to a short beard) (that of Lenin's).

The means of art… (in view of perfection).

We thought that the Marxist critique *gave* the key to explaining history past and present.

We found wonderful examples of virtue, of devotion, of enthusiasm and of the capacity of work, of efficiency, of disinterestedness, of being set free, in the branches and the individuals of the party. The coldness and the ruthless critique also attracted us. Like the sacrifices asked of taste and sentiment, even of individual intelligence. The a posteriori critique of intelligent conclusions and of our own "texts" strongly enticed us. It appeared to resemble the critique of texts by *Time*. This is only *one* viewpoint of the artist that we are. (The artist does not refuse a single critical viewpoint whatsoever).

But we came to find many things: that the ad hominem critique (economistic critique) is worth no more than the psychological critique, that it engenders a grotesque and criminal pretension, that it stifles instinct, the intelligence of the heart.

1. *Killing,* desire, impulse.

2. Creating a dried-out pretension, a ridiculous and trying rigorism.

LES FLEURYS, APRIL 8 1950.

We will not look for anything (to say) about what is "significant" about our epoch (this will work itself out on its own; we are all too immersed in it).

We will search (on the contrary) for what does not appear as significant, what does not return to its symbols (into its symbolism): whereof serial time (or eternity) is.

We have to resay "mute nature in heavy ranks that surrounds us", takes us by the shoulders again, cloaks us, coifs and cravats us, we have to resay April (or October).

Here then I am returned to the sentiments that made me write *Ad litem*,
minus the despair. This here, these forms taken by mute nature, is all at once terrible, absurd, discouraging, but lives, embroiders, continues. And alright: all the better (and all the worse); the question is not there.

Here, where a whole landscape grabs me by the collar, extends my shoulders to the right and to the left, o solitude encumbered by mutes each one fixed to their place and without looking, paralytic, and having nought to express itself (where I do not have all that much to defend myself from dangerous animals) but my voice, here I feel my reason for being again.

The landscape ∞[1] of big sooted knots, numb and paralytic (infirm) under the bluish overshadowing, the voluminous worries coming westerly.

---

1 Replacing the lyrical o with the arithmetical symbol of infinity ∞ (the setting 8)

LES FLEURYS, 8 APRIL 1950.

The arts and letters do not conceive themselves, are not born and do not live but by the illusion of communication and sympathy. This is (this illusion (this lily)) but a vegetation and flowering, conceivable only in peace (cf. Lucretius, Book V)

Sympathy and communication do not "find" themselves but in love and in festivals, in the ravishment, *in the illusion itself* that allows life to continue (coitus).

Neither in critique nor in judgment (in *war*, ideological or material, terror)

So that one is not ABLE to legitimately communicate but the ravishment or else one kills. The ravishment alone communicates itself. In any case, it is not according to our taste to communicate anger and judgement...

Now, supposing one *loses* this illusion (leading to suicide), there is still only one form of legitimate suicide: that is (joyous) devotion and love, rising to speak, in praise. Look who is closing the circle and turning back to speak again, to art: to letters.

PROEM.

LES FLEURYS, APRIL 9-10 1950.

(This one is very imperfect, to return to.)

I am not through, have nothing but incomplete *ideas* (incompletely stated) and it is not so much about them than it is about completing them.

They are like fierce birds of passage whose form I regret not having been able to know entirely, or rather more like lightning bolts, since their singular virtue is, above all, it seems to me, in illuminating the conscience. They (these ideas) illuminate the conscience, but I will always have the sentiment of *chance* in their spark, whose removal from my eyes costs me nearly all. Moreover, what good is it to get them to reproduce? To know and make known my *opinion*, the opinion of this very instant? But I know full well that it could be negated, tomorrow, or the following instant, by some (contradictory) idea that I will be dealt in the same way...

That would be their *beauty* itself then? or even more

so their only quality, to know the being of "thoughts"? (here is a rare and precious thing (what a wonder, a thought!!!!)...

But what is essential, is it not the gleam, the illumination of conscience? And what does the lightning itself matter then, its form, its arborescence, since what follows it will have the same effect (will produce a similar gleaming). And yet *it will be followed* (there is the point, the reason for my disinterest or laziness).

LES FLEURYS, APRIL 10 1950.

This infirmity I recognize in my thoughts is one of the reasons for my partiality (for things). For by proposing to me a defined, existing object that endures outside my conscience, I could well suffer not getting it every time that I apply myself to it, every time an incomplete idea, a brief gleaming, inasmuch as *it* in effect, however it, endures and persists (unlike a state of the soul, a sentiment, a passion), and the incomplete ideas that come to me in turn, relating itself always to *it*, will be partially valid once again, and that finally the sum, the accumulation of these gleamings or incomplete touches, will be able to give a sufficiently voluminous (solid) approximation of said object, will at last be able *to verify* itself there.

And certainly, I concede that this infirmity would be particular to me, that others suffer nothing the like, and receive on the contrary perfect (or complete) ideas that they are able to note down straightaway (to formulate them in their perfection). Those ones should know of wondrous satisfactions! Those ones alone are perhaps worthy of the name thinkers or poets (or writers).

With them there is no stammering at all, no such thing as an inferiority complex. Ah! they should never be unhappy.

And as for myself, the exercise that I propose for myself, or rather the exercises which I submit myself to, are not but so as to earn, one day, to attain, one day, such a command, such an assurance, such a hand-turn tomorrow.

Undoubtedly it is the reason why I continue to exert myself, to write, why my *work* continues. But if I were to have acquired this skill, virtuosity, would I continue to *produce* masterworks? I ask myself this.

–Yes, undoubtedly, for the objects delight me, they interest me inasmuch as I will be forever happy to grasp them anew, and I will have them forever anew to grasp, to execute them with a handturn. What enjoyments!

But I doubt that this would ever be granted to me.

Whoever does not satisfy themselves with images, metaphors, symbols, is naturally only visited by incomplete ideas (as if they were inhibited at every instant (in the course of their formulation) not so much as by an impotence of the subject (of the author), but by an opposition ("at minimum" (e.g.)) of the object (and therefore by a scrupling of the subject).

In order to speak with happiness and authority, to have complete thoughts, one must be under the influence, one must be the object of a strong sentiment.

Yet whoever does not have sentiments but as delight in the strangeness of things (by relation to the merry-go-round of our sentiments), who is not delighted but by the margin between the reality of the object and the expression (generally pictographic) we can give it, this one knows the just mentioned inhibition at once and (I want to believe) the chance to get off the merry-go-round (little by little) to do original work: the originality coming from the object, not from the subject.

Here is where I rejoin what I already wrote of the *differential quality*, more interesting than the analogic quality.

In sum, the objects finally created (poems, paintings) will then manifest two kinds of qualities at once:

1. the moral qualities of the author (these scruples, this humility, tenacity)

2. the differential quality of the object.

I am not far from believing (and duly) that is the culmination of art, touching beauty.

Not that touching here merely signifies piteous, and that beauty comes only by a constant mishap, constantly surpassed (by the same mistake).

Perfection is suddenly able to come to those objects – unforeseeably – by insertion, the emergence all at once of a supplementary quality, unheard of, new, which self-induces all at once in this cage, this cloth of (prudent) mistakes and illuminates it, conferring life upon it. Then the water comes from all sides. This comes alive then, to beat (as when the amoeba disencysts itself), to pulse.

"To woven cloth, god sends the thread."

Note from 12-18-50: Naturally, in writing the preceding, I was not thinking of Cézanne. Rereading this eight months later, I think of him immediately.

•

The resurrection in *Music* (in the Greek sense) is unforeseeable. But it is only in these conditions (never sought for itself) that it is able to produce itself.

IV
CAPITAL PROEM

LES FLEURYS, APRIL 10 1950.

Of the one part, you, humans, with your civilizations, your journals, your artists, your poets, your passions, sentiments, the whole human world finally more and more revolting, unbearable (unjudgeable).

And of the other part, the rest: the mutes, mute nature, the open country, the seas and all the objects and the animals and the vegetables. Not bad things, as one sees. At last all the rest.

•

It is this second part perfectly outside of humans, that is
my reason for being
to represent, unto which I give voice.

What I would like (to make itself heard by my voice) to make itself speak as highly as humans.

It would suffice to say one word in order to dominate all the rest with ease.

One sees that I am not terribly anxious about my rank among the poets, among humans: it is not about that. The armoire would like to speak at last: that is all.

You...

You are there, all around me – today, you trees, pebbles of the orchard, clouds in the sky, wondrous dead nature, uncontested nature.

You are there,

You are there indeed!

Indisputably. Rising or setting, dead or alive, strong, present,

We will speak to them, to the humans.

So, to take on their voice, their speech. Let us speak! You speak! I am your interpreter. Say what you have to say. Say only what you are.

Go on say it to me.

I am interested only in you.

You devour my life entirely, my speech.

Long exercised, since my youth, in this.

....

THE PEAR-TREES.

LES FLEURYS, APRIL 10 1950, AFTERNOON.

(These are the pear-trees that are given to you in today's human terms.)

Look how the pear-trees today want to speak themselves. The lower part of the orchard's register is ruled. The trunks and main branches are spelled out slowly there, with application. The higher part rests unspent, reserved for vernal liberty.

Their writing (in the orchard) on the trellis is rather slow, a little higher up than it is round, strongly applied, irregular enough, knotted, twisted and trembling; right there for the trunk, the branches and branchettes. (What suffices right there, for etc.)

Launching themselves from there into the springtime of sticklets (rodlets) (vectors) in thriving vertically a lot more quickly, decidedly; throwing from right and left quick projectiles of leaves, carried through quickly, realized; all the same; as one mails wingtips, and "et ceteras", to occupy the air, as flank-guards (or as one quickly occupies a devolved space, to assure one's breathing). Like the wondrous antlers of reindeer or stags. The pear-trees are the stags of the vegetable patch, of the orchard. These are little pennants and (spinning) spoons all at once. Et cetera.

Thus, they activate rodlets in all possible directions, while still in season. One will see those that one passes over again (will come back to for several recollections) to put it in broad strokes, one will see this later on. It is the concern of another season.

At the same time, at the very beginning of said season, in several places (as well as from the trunk itself, as main branches or weeds) they raise up bouquets, that is to say what matters most to them—and that in exact number, but quite variable, which signifies the year's power of production. Carefully, lovingly grouped and clothed and presented in white costumes and ceremonial roses, of ravishing, tempting, adorable, frail (and not so fragile as that) bouquets of reddening tendrils. *Lacking the color (ink and brush of tender green, then darker.)* Where then, at least in some of them, God knows what takes place, in their little open (frilled) breeches (corollas), God knows what mysterious coitus, bee kisses, or simple orgasm of individual and solitary nerves, or pollination by air, by the tremoring of petals or pistils in the zephyr or some automatic deglutition in the sun (they are so sensible, so swelled up, these little clitorises, these vulvas so swelled up, the bared mucous membrane! Anything is able to make them play, is able to pollinate them.)

Seasonal ingenuity.

Just as soon the whole comedy of tender colors ceases (until new order), the petals are cleared, thrown on top of the chair, or the ground, or abandoned to the air. It will be about swelling up *that thing*, slowly, carefully, under the protection and diversion (the vulgar ballet of diversion) of the leaves, more and more arrogant and familiar, in a more and more numerous population in droves around the bandstands.

To swell up *that thing?* What, *this thing ? – The pear* (whose question will be for another time).

It has its bottom wreathlet, the little pear, etc. (paragraph to swell up, to nourish, to water, to sweeten all the way to the seeds that are to be put there, which gives you the true taste of the tree, a bit bland).

And all this comes to fruition seriously in the orchard, in the overshadowing bluish atmosphere of gusting wind, or in the great momentary aestival ecstasies of a sun which does not jest, which executes more or less punctually, but always brutally, its function.

The big fruit-trees in *your* regions (people of the temperate septentrion), are the most knotty, short, squat, twisted. Truly, that is why they are often sharpened to a point, cut up, amputated to keep the fruit's sap. These are stubbed and infirm. Slow to (enter into) function. Armored like turtles or certain prehistoric animals.

As for their fruit (pears, apples, plums), these have come out to be but a bit more than berries.

THE EGG.

LES FLEURYS, APRIL 10 1950.

Who makes (avows) (produces and entrusts to the exterior) eggs? – the scaled or feathered animals (after being straddled). God knows why. Those ones are able to *confide* their eggs. The others guard their eggs to the interior, and bear to the world, to secret ovarian history, nearly fulfilled individuals. (One does not show it, one is not able to confide it.)

•

Ah! branchlets, sticklets, bundlets, rodlets, *you* foliate, leaf through.

You: pronouns, bourgeons.

Foliate, etc.: the verb of the second person plural: in the present imperative and indicative (And besides this deploys itself, infoliates itself (R, S, E, T) (ar, ess, e, tee)

•

The trees in bloom (notably the fruit-trees) (pear-trees etc.) are arranged like genealogical trees (the marriages are represented there by each flower bouquet) in serial time (in eternity).

•

Sacred character (for the bourgeois paysans) the vernal, (flowering,) fruit-trees: one will not cut them for vases, nor for church (like those of boxwood)!

It is disgraceful to cut them (perhaps the city dwellers ignore it? No! They are not able to ignore it!)

On the contrary, they are indeed to be cut before winter. It is a rite, rather useful.

•

To put the Greek or Roman (pagan) spirit into all of this. The living nature of its *diverse* divinities. The harmony of *a great number* of gods and goddesses.

The earth offers all this, the arms extending out into trees and bouquets. Boreas, the winds, the sun (Phoebus) pass underneath or resplendish. Veritable symphony, orchestra. All ordering itself, rhythming itself. All characters. All characters (none are forgotten) of a wondrous sacred ballet (expressing all at once; a diversity, a wondrous richness). Grace, harmony, joy, sadness and harmonious sorrows. And all this here, in a world *reduced* (one has no idea of anything else but the Mediterranean, even the Aegean Sea).

•

Of course, not to *put* the *Greek* spirit there. But to *forget the Christian spirit,* here is what is important.

So, to antidote it, from the Greek (for example).

....

CONFIRMATION OF THE PEAR-TREES

LES FLEURYS, APRIL 12 1950 (NIGHT).

Retaking up the outlined pear-trees today it seems evident to me (what, I had been so blind!) that their knotted "writing", the *form* of their trunks, branches and reams is the consequence of severe, rigorous, successive amputation to which they are submitted (for their regular *pruning*). They were rigorously trimmed, erased. There is a certain relationship of amputation, of *erasure*, to stumps, *then* of stumps to large fruit (large pears).

•

Thus, often, when one trims (practices amputation on) the language (a sentence), certain words that remain take on this character (trunks or branches of pear-trees): it then seems as though the quill were being passed over to them again, that they were confirming themselves.

In any case, the look of the reader *must*, in their turn, of all necessity, pass over these words often, due to the abstruse way of the text: overly concise, clashed. These words, these parts of the text, swell up interiorly, regain strength *but* come out knotty, cut up. They are confirming. They are confirmed.

They become thicker, knottier charged besides with sense (and the possibility of flowers and fruits). For in trimming something, one automatically confirms what remains.

This genre of style (like that of the pear-trees) makes strong *writing* (more writing than speaking) (cf. Mallarmé).

Right there the rhetoric of the pear-tree.

What is especially interesting in these trees, is this: from these confirmed stumps (from those old and infirm, arthritic) the bouquets of first communicants or brides are born. From the twisted black, the white and the roseate.

All that has not been cut, is passed over there, once again, every spring. This takes on a terribly engorged character. All that accumulates there infuses itself directly, by the shortest peduncle, in the pear, that blows up beautifully.

•

This confirmation, the mosses still confirm it in attaching themselves to these trunks and limbs as to old rocks (old rock-work), and much more readily to the much older and thicker trunks of smooth trees.

•

The word *certes* expresses these confirmed parts of the pear-trees well enough.

LES FLEURYS, THURSDAY APRIL 13 1950.

It is the fifteenth day of our stay in this countryside. The healthy and tranquil life I have led there, the raw impressions I received as soon as I arrived (Nioque of the Early-Spring), also the fact of my readings reduced here happily to several books I found again: a small scholarly anthology of ancient literatures (Greek and Latin: Theocritus, Lucretius, Virgil), another rough summary of the poets of the XIXth C. (until 1850), an abridged history of modern time (Humanism and Reform; I drafted the project of one day writing a history from 1490 to our present day), the general disposition wherein I find myself finally since detaching completely from P, my experience with S regarding the collection of delinquent tribute, my associations reduced to Braque, that whole cast of circumstances; moreover, ventilated by the effect of physiological and intellectual cleansing of the early-spring's fresh hydrotherapy that has granted me three or four days of taking one or two new steps intellectually, I believe, in knowing myself, and thus in my *project* (of better grasping my project).

Right here in what sense that is.

Novum organum.

For some time now I have been asking myself whether I should not work toward developing a *declaration* of my experiences and of the moral and aesthetic I believe I have achieved.

More and more avidly I ponder a work of this genre. This declaration will signal my philosophical evolution, will point out the reason of my works, rectifying what was said of them (worries of language, worries as to rationalist philosophy, idea of the artist's Destiny).

DECLARATION, CONDITION,AND FATE OF THE ARTIST

LES FLEURYS, APRIL 14 1950.

Novum organum.

I. To consider the artist as a researcher (desirous, fierce, ravished) who finds at times, a disinterested laborer.

(Hence the aesthetic of feeling one's way, of resayings, etc. *(Notebook of the pinewood).* To transcend the analogic magma and the same allegory. To achieve clear formulation. Without too many resayings, without too many explanations.) Virtue of authentic research given as such.

Who finds at times, but is not interested in their findings as such: they continue to search.

Human of the laboratory: laboratory of expression. Starting 1. from raw material, the emotions it gives, of desire it inspires 2. from its means of expression.

They are a (whole) human like any other.

They do not *seek* to be a *witness* either: they are one. They raise their means of expression.

Express *facing the world* (apropos of emotions they receive from it) *their most particular.* Respect their first impression: what they receive from the objects of the world. This has to count for far more than anything: no other shame. They are there to express mute nature (the mystery, the secret, as the scholar's equal).

New conceptions of the artist as before the furnishing of weapons, proverbs (gratuitous proverbs, of the eternal) (Expression of Blin's regarding Artaud: flashing weapons.)

II. This idea of the artist is new.

It follows from the progress of the sciences (theory of relativity), of functionalization (Kafka), new social revolutions (communism, technocracy), new ethnologic discoveries (African, primal civilizations),

—from the myth of the new human: from the notion of *human* relativity (Surrealism, Marxism, Freudism). The human is an animal as any other is. Their proper function

—from the death of God.

The artist sums up science, abolishes it, brings life back to the surface, expresses the total world.

Rejoices, recreates the human. Effect of catastrophies and upheavals: wars, atrocities, new barbarism.

•

The new humanism:

Philosophy of philosophies. Psychology of art.

Museums. The taste of the ancient.

The abhumanism of the artist.

•

They are unable to be but revolutionary, yet also unable but to maintain *values.*

Must transcend the philosophical and religious parties (Rabelais, Montaigne, around 1530-1550: non-protestants, not brought down by unrest: smiling or laughing.)

A single solution: to express mute nature

in marking its means of expression, treating it without shame (for this one must have the resources).
A certain senility: naiveté refound
to restart from stammering, from zero.

•

To transcend classicism and romanticism by the primacy given to the matter, to the object, to the unheard of qualities that go out from it;
what Braque names the fortuitous (or the fatal?); by this third term: the object.

•

What we reclaim for them, for this worker, this researcher: a new Collège de France (to remember the grounds for its creation by François I[st]: secularization of "research".)

EXPLANATION TO THOSE WHO MATTER TO ME (THAT IS TO SAY TO THOSE WHO LOVE ME OR WILL LOVE ME...)

LES FLEURYS, APRIL 15 1950.

If, for quite some time, I have taken to the habit of dating every one of my manuscripts in my head the very moment that I start them, more than anything that is because I have come to such doubt as to their quality, or to such uncertainty when considering them as to their relation to "truth" or "beauty", as to the partial that could be drawn from them, I consider them all, without exception, as *documents* first, and if I do not manage to draw a "definitive" work from them, (it should be possible to explain this word, to say which qualities are requirable of a work meriting that it not be dated), I want to be able to retain them in my keep (or even publish them) in their exact *chronological order.*

NIOQUE OF THE EARLY SPRING.

PARIS, APRIL 22-23 1950.

Westerly come huge worries, bluish overshadowing, in gusts (loading (occupying) of a turbulent setting) at the top (the two upper thirds) of the page, and at times soaking it completely, dampening, at times sprinkling all the way to the reader (in their window frame).

(All the space between the reader and the page elsewhere swept across by the wind (full flow) whipping full force)

(Plenitude of all this: as full as my own body.)

A NOTE FOR THE GNOQUE.

MAY 29, 1953 UPON AWAKING.

The countryside, in an open collar and large tie.

NIOQUE OF THE EARLY SPRING.

PARIS, JUNE 6, 1953.

It is westerly, that is to say in gusts from the right, that the frigid worries, the bluish overshadowing, come to us. And at times even flurries of hailstone.

We look readily to midday;

Our dramatics come to us westerly.

....

ACKNOWLEDGMENTS

Excerpts of *Nioque of the Early-Spring* appeared first in *The Brooklyn Rail* and *Pen Poetry Series*. Grateful acknowledgment is given to the editors Donald Breckenridge and Danniel Schoonebeek.

A big thank you to Alan Felsenthal and Ben Estes for bringing this project into the open as a book.

And many, many thank yous to Wendy Xu for the attentive and enduring reading and support.

OTHER TITLES FROM THE SONG CAVE

1. *A Dark Dreambox of Another Kind* by **Alfred Starr Hamilton**
2. *My Enemies* by **Jane Gregory**
3. *Rude Woods* by **Nate Klug**
4. *Georges Braque and Others* by **Trevor Winkfield**
5. *The Living Method* by **Sara Nicholson**
6. *Splash State* by **Todd Colby**
7. *Essay Stanzas* by **Thomas Meyer**
8. *Illustrated Games of Patience* by **Ben Estes**
9. *Dark Green* by **Emily Hunt**
10. *Honest James* by **Christian Schlegel**
11. *M* by **Hannah Brooks-Motl**
12. *What the Lyric Is* by **Sara Nicholson**
13. *The Hermit* by **Lucy Ives**
14. *The Orchid Stories* by **Kenward Elmslie**
15. *Do Not Be a Gentleman When You Say Goodnight* by **Mitch Sisskind**
16. *HAIRDO* by **Rachel B. Glaser**
17. *Motor Maids across the Continent* by **Ron Padgett**
18. *Songs for Schizoid Siblings* by **Lionel Ziprin**

19. *Professionals of Hope*, The Selected Writings of **Subcomandante Marcos**
20. *Fort Not* by **Emily Skillings**
21. *Riddles, Etc.* by **Geoffrey Hilsabeck**
22. *CHARAS: The Improbable Dome Builders*, by **Syeus Mottel** (Co-published with Pioneer Works)
23. *Yeah No* by **Jane Gregory**